Read & Resp

FOR
KS1

SECTION 1

Amazing Grace

SECTION 2

Guided reading

SECTION 3

Shared reading

SECTION 4

Plot, character and setting

SECTION 5

Talk about it

SECTION 6

Get writing

SECTION 7

Assessment

PAGE 1

Read & Respond

FOR KS1

Author: Jean Evans

Editor: Pam Kelt

Assistant Editor: Marion Archer

Series Designer: Anna Oliwa

Designer: Liz Gilbert

Illustrations: Caroline Binch/
Jon Mitchell/Beehive Illustration

Text © Jean Evans © 2009 Scholastic Ltd

Designed using Adobe InDesign

Published by Scholastic Ltd, Villiers House,
Clarendon Avenue, Leamington Spa,
Warwickshire CV32 5PR

www.scholastic.co.uk

Printed by Bell & Bain

1 2 3 4 5 6 7 8 9   9 0 1 2 3 4 5

British Library Cataloguing-in-Publication Data
A catalogue record for this book is available from the British
Library.

ISBN 978-1407-11239-8

Acknowledgements
The publishers would like to thank **Frances Lincoln** for the use of
text and illustrations from *Amazing Grace* by Mary Hoffman text
© 1991, Mary Hoffman, illustrations © 1991, Caroline Binch
(1991, Frances Lincoln). Every effort has been made to trace
copyright holders for the works published in this book, and the
publishers apologise for any inadvertent omissions.

Amazing Grace

About the book

Amazing Grace is a heart-warming story featuring a popular girl who adores stories. Grace loves listening to stories, reading them to herself or making them up in her head. Often Grace acts out the stories she enjoys. She makes her own props and costumes and involves her friends and her cat, Paw-Paw. Grace never minds whether the parts are for girls or boys. She plays them all.

When her teacher asks who would like to be Peter Pan in the school play, Grace is very keen. However, her friends think otherwise and tell her she cannot be Peter because she is not a boy and she is black. This does not put off Grace because she is determined to play her favourite character. Nana helps Grace to realise that she can do anything if she puts her mind to it by taking her to see a ballerina performing in *Romeo and Juliet* at the theatre.

When Grace auditions for the part of Peter Pan, everyone is thrilled by her performance and the part is hers. The play is a huge success and Grace's dream comes true.

Amazing Grace is an example of a story with a familiar setting. Children will be able to empathise with Grace when friends at school express opinions that hurt her, and rejoice with her when she receives praise for her excellent performance. The importance of family support is emphasised as Grace turns to Nana and Ma to discuss her feelings. Above all, this book will help to develop children's self-confidence and encourage them to feel good about their own contributions to peer and family groups.

About the author

Mary Hoffman studied English Literature at Newnham College, Cambridge and her first book was published in 1975 as *White Magic*. Since then she has written around 90 books for children, including the *Amazing Grace* picture book stories.

Mary modelled the character of Grace on herself, for she too was a girl who loved stories and acting. The first book about Grace appeared in 1991 and there are now picture books, big books, chapter-books, dolls and videos based on this popular character. Other Grace stories include *Grace and Family*, *Starring Grace*, *Encore Grace!*, *Bravo Grace!* and *Princess Grace*. Of all her books, those featuring Grace generate the most fan mail.

Mary Hoffman is married with three grown-up daughters and lives with her husband in a big old converted barn near Oxford. Among her other many book titles are *An Angel Just Like Me*, *Three Wise Women*, *The Colour of Home*, and *City of Masks*, *City of Stars* and *City of Flowers* from the *Stravaganza* series for older readers.

Facts and figures

Amazing Grace has sold more than 1.5 million copies. In 1992 *Amazing Grace* was selected for Children's Book of the Year, Commended for the Kate Greenaway Medal and added to the National Curriculum Reading List, becoming an international best-seller.

Its sequel, *Grace and Family* was among *Junior Education's* Best Books of 1995 and shortlisted for the Sheffield Libraries Book Award 1996.

There are dual language versions of *Amazing Grace*, including Bengali/English; Gujurati/English; Panjabi/English and Urdu/English. In 2008, Coventry County Council short-listed it as part of its Coventry Inspiration Book Awards.

Guided reading

Introducing the book

Introduce the book, and refer to the title, cover, pages, illustrations and blurb to make predictions about the story.

Begin by exploring the illustration on the front cover together. Look at the main image of Grace and ask the children to describe her appearance. Discuss her hair and skin colour, her clothes and jewellery. Talk about how she is losing her milk teeth and probably has lots of wobbly teeth. Does that help us to determine how old she might be? Encourage the children to make comparisons with their own appearances and those of their friends. Draw attention to the less prominent image behind depicting Grace dancing. Do these images help us to decide what the story might be about?

Read the title and ask questions about it. *Who is Amazing Grace? Might she be the girl on the cover? Why do you think she is 'amazing'? Do you know anyone or anything that is 'amazing'?*

Draw attention to Mary Hoffman's name and explain that she is the author of the book. Encourage the children to name the authors of some of their favourite books. Read out the name Caroline Binch, explain that she is the illustrator and discuss the work of an illustrator. Find out more about Mary Hoffman and Caroline Binch to extend this discussion by turning to the first page of *Amazing Grace*. (Section 1 of this book, *Read and Respond – Amazing Grace*, also includes information about Mary Hoffman.)

Turn to the back cover and read the blurb to give the children an outline of the plot. In the light of this information, encourage the children to comment again about the content of the story.

Initial reading

The first time that you share *Amazing Grace* with the children, focus on making the experience enjoyable. Read clearly and expressively, encouraging participation, either by joining in, asking questions or listening with interest. Indicate words by moving along them with a finger or pointer as you read, and remember to pause at significant points to ask the children what they think will happen next or to predict a word or phrase. Ask: *What do you think Grace will do now? Do you think Grace's friends will vote for her or for someone else?*

As you continue to read, ensure that the children understand the text through appropriate comments and queries. For example: *The teacher is holding an audition. Do you know what an audition is?* If necessary, give a clear explanation by describing a simplified version of the event in a familiar context, such as choosing a child for a specific task.

Encourage the children to empathise with Grace by making links with their own experiences through appropriate questions. Ask: *Have you ever felt rejected? Can you say when? Have people ever made unkind comments about you? Did anything happen to make you feel better?*

Always be prepared to follow the children's comments, interests and ideas, for example, when they talk about how they would react in similar situations. Draw attention to the importance of illustrations in enhancing the story and emphasise them.

Finally, encourage the children to share their initial opinions about it. Stress that not everyone will have the same responses, and that some people will like particular aspects while others will dislike them. Comment, too, that opinions can change on re-reading the book.

Subsequent readings

Once the children are familiar with the book, and have shared the enjoyment of a first reading, carefully plan further readings to focus on different aspects to extend their comprehension of the text, to develop fluency in reading aloud and to increase their word and sentence level objectives. Teach the children to:

● use a range of decoding strategies for unfamiliar words, check for meaning and correct errors by themselves

● build up words and understand spelling patterns in context

- read high frequency words on sight
- develop understanding of sentence construction and punctuation
- read aloud with pace and expression appropriate to the grammar of the text
- track the text from left to right and word by word
- understand and use book and print related terms correctly
- identify story elements (plot, character, setting)
- predict and infer
- sequence story events.

Setting the scene

Ask the children to read the story together up to the reference to Doctor Grace, describing Grace's love of stories and acting. Encourage them to use a combination of phonic knowledge, picture cues and re-reading of sentences to do so. Pose questions to help them determine how this section of the book sets the scene for the story. Ask: *What two things does Grace love?* (Answer: stories and acting.) *Can you think of some of the ways Grace enjoys stories? Can you remember some of the characters Grace likes to dress up as? Who has the most exciting part when Grace acts out the stories? Who else takes part?*

Invite the children to extend this scene setting with sentence ideas of their own about alternative stories that Grace could re-enact. Ask about characters that she would play and props that she would need.

Choosing Peter Pan

Move from setting the scene to considering a main event of the story, for example, talking about parts for the forthcoming production of *Peter Pan*. Read the discussion with Grace, her teacher and her friends at school, and the following conversation with her family at home. Re-enact the scene together, focusing on the actions and voices.

Encourage the children to use picture cues for actions and draw attention to punctuation that indicates how to read the text, such as speech marks, italics, pauses (a row of dots), vocabulary ('whispered') and question marks. Discuss how the words indicate the moods of the characters, for example, 'sad', 'angry', 'cheered up', and modify voices accordingly.

Read the final sentence of this section and talk about how it leads the reader into the next story event. (Nana tells Grace that she can do anything if she puts her mind to it and then takes her to the theatre to inspire her further.)

You can do it!

Read the section of the book about Grace's visit to the theatre with Nana and the next page where she is pretending to be Juliet. Invite the children to think of words and phrases to describe how Grace is feeling as she approaches the theatre and anticipates the forthcoming performance. Ask what she might be thinking as she looks at the signs and posters on the walls. Look at the pictures of Grace pretending to be Juliet after her visit to the ballet, and read the text. Ask: *How does the visit to the ballet make Grace even more determined to fulfil her ambition to be Peter Pan?* Recall the expression Nana uses to encourage Grace in her pursuit of this aim. ("'You can be anything you want, Grace, if you put your mind to it.'")

Achieving the ambition

Read the page about the audition and ask the children to describe Grace's performance, using the text and illustration to help. Ask: *Who was chosen for the main parts? Did Grace achieve her ambition?* Turn the page and look at the illustration of Grace playing Peter Pan. Encourage the children to describe how Grace is dressed and the expression on her face. Read the text on the opposite page and identify which words describe the play and Grace's contribution ('a great success', 'amazing'). Ask: *How did Grace feel after her performance?* ("I feel as if I could fly all the way home!'") Invite the children to think of alternative words to express this feeling of elation.

Guided reading

The story ends with a comment by Nana ("'If Grace put her mind to it – she can do anything she want.'"). Read this together and talk about the importance of repeating this comment here, to the story as a whole, and to the creation of a satisfying ending.

Book review

After discussing the story, characters and specific events in detail, invite the children to give their overall impression of the book through personal responses. Ask appropriate questions and give positive encouragement to help them to voice their opinions with confidence and clarity. Ask: *What was the story about? Did you enjoy it? What was your favourite event in the story? Was there any part of the story that you did not enjoy? Who is the main character? Is there anything that you particularly liked or disliked about her? Can you say why you feel like this? Were there any other characters that you liked or disliked?*

Encourage the children to empathise with the feelings of the characters in the book, again through careful questioning. Ask how Grace felt at different points in the story, for example, when she was playing a favourite character, when her friends said that she was not suitable for the part of Peter Pan or when she achieved her ambition. Talk about Nana's feelings, and the feelings of the other children. Try to encourage the children to understand how their own experiences help them to 'feel' the emotions of the characters when they are reading a story.

Shared reading

Extract 1

● Display an enlarged copy of the extract, covering the words relating to the ways that Grace enjoyed stories: 'read', 'told', 'made', 'books', 'TV', 'films', 'video' and 'memory'. Invite the children to read the text, pausing to predict the missing words using cues from the extract and existing grammatical knowledge.

● Ask the children to identify the sentences in the extract by circling the capital letters at the start and full stops at the end of each one. Ask if there are any other capital letters in the extract.

Discuss how capital letters are also used for names, and abbreviations such as 'TV'.

● Invite the children to find two similar sentences in the extract ('Grace was a girl who loved stories' and 'Grace just loved stories'). Discuss how the author has repeated these words to emphasise an important aspect of the story.

● Explore the accompanying illustration and discuss how it links with, and adds detail to, the text.

Extract 2

● Display an enlarged copy of the extract and ask the children to identify punctuation that informs us that someone is speaking. Underline the direct speech, using a different colour for each character. Identify what each character says and use contextual clues to decide how to say these words, for example, Raj might speak in a raised voice to emphasise his point whereas the teacher might speak in a quiet, calm voice to ensure she has the children's attention. Ask the class which word describes how Natalie speaks ('whispered').

● Invite the children to add new words to the text to describe how Raj, Natalie and the teacher might speak, for example, 'loudly', 'quietly' or 'calmly'. Read the revised extract using different voices for each character.

● Explore the accompanying illustration and discuss how it extends information given in the extract (the appearance of the classroom and of Grace and her friends).

● Draw attention to the italics used for *Peter Pan* and explain that titles of books, plays and poems are often indicated in this way.

Extract 3

● Display an enlarged copy of the extract and read it together. Discuss information in the text about how Grace and Nana travelled to the theatre (bus and train). Ask the children to add descriptive words to help the reader to imagine the journey more clearly, for example, 'overcrowded bus', 'swaying, rattling train', and to find the word that describes the theatre ('grand'). Suggest that the children find alternative words, for example, 'magnificent' or 'fine'. Discuss how the words 'beautiful sparkling lights' help the reader to imagine the theatre sign.

● Ask the children to find the exclamation

mark after the word 'JULIET!', explain that this indicates that it should be read with emphasis and invite them to read it with this in mind.

● Find the question, 'Are we going to the ballet, Nana?', and take turns to point to the question mark. Read the question aloud, modulating the voice to make the words sound like a question. Make up different questions starting with the words 'Are we….?'

● Discuss how capital letters are used for the words describing the theatre signs to make them the same as those on the accompanying illustration. As a class design a poster for a show and write key words in capitals.

Extract 1

Grace was a girl who loved stories. She didn't mind if they were read to her or told to her or made up in her own head. She didn't care if they were from books or on TV or in films or on the video or out of Nana's long memory. Grace just loved stories.

And after she had heard them, or sometimes while they were still going on, Grace would act them out. And she always gave herself the most exciting part.

Text extract © 1991, Mary Hoffman; illustration © 1991, Caroline Binch.

Extract 2

One day at school her teacher said they were going to do the play of *Peter Pan*. Grace put up her hand to be…Peter Pan.

"You can't be called Peter," said Raj. "That's a boy's name."

But Grace kept her hand up.

"You can't be Peter Pan," whispered Natalie. "He wasn't black." But Grace kept her hand up.

"All right," said the teacher. "Lots of you want to be Peter Pan, so we'll have to have auditions. We'll choose the parts next Monday."

Text extract © 1991, Mary Hoffman; illustration © 1991, Caroline Binch.

Extract 3

Next day was Saturday and Nana told Grace they were going out. In the afternoon they caught a bus and a train into town. Nana took Grace to a grand theatre. Outside it said, "ROSALIE WILKINS in ROMEO AND JULIET" in beautiful sparkling lights.

"Are we going to the ballet, Nana?" asked Grace.

"We are, Honey, but I want you to look at these pictures first."

Nana showed Grace some photographs of a beautiful young girl dancer in a tutu. "STUNNING NEW JULIET!" it said on one of them.

Text extract © 1991, Mary Hoffman; illustration © 1991, Caroline Binch.

Plot, character and setting

We are amazing

Objective: To create short simple texts on paper and on screen that combine words with images (and sounds).
What you need: Copies of *Amazing Grace*, fantasy costumes and props, digital camera, printer, small and large sheets of paper, two large sheets of card, hole punch, ribbon scissors and writing materials.
Cross-curricular links: Drama.

What to do

● Read *Amazing Grace* and discuss the fantasy roles that Grace likes to play. Ask: *What sort of costumes does she wear? What props does she use?*
● Explore some costumes and props and talk about the roles they might be used for. Ask the children to choose costumes to dress up in, and props to bring their role to life.
● Invite the children to photograph one another adopting suitable poses for their chosen roles and print out the results. Suggest that they use the photographs in a book entitled *We are amazing*.
● Cut around individual photographs and stick them to the top of large sheets of paper to form pages. Ask the children to write a sentence underneath about why they are amazing.
● Using the card create a book cover, adding the title, a photograph montage and children's drawings. Punch holes in the cover and pages, and thread ribbon through to finish the book.
● Write a contents page together, indicating the names of each child and the roles that they play.

Differentiation
For older/more confident learners: Ask the children to work in small groups to create a book about a favourite story, using the same process.
For younger/less confident learners: Help the children to dress up, and support them with appropriate vocabulary to describe their roles.

Who am I?

Objective: To explain their views to others in a small group, decide how to report the group's views to the class.
What you need: Several copies of *Amazing Grace*, photocopiable page 15 (one copy for each child, one larger version) and writing materials.

What to do

● Ask the children to name the main character in the story. Ask: *Who else is an important character?* Explain that they are going to build up character profiles of Grace and Nana, and discuss the meaning of 'character' and 'profile'.
● Invite the children to work in pairs to discuss Grace's appearance and what is special about her. Suggest that they refer to *Amazing Grace* for words and phrases to support their comments, for example, Grace was determined – "'I can be anything I want'". Also encourage them to explore the illustrations to help with descriptive words relating to appearance.
● Display a large version of photocopiable page 15 on the board. Write down the children's suggested words to describe Grace's character and appearance in the appropriate boxes.
● Ask the children, still in pairs, to discuss Nana's appearance and character, using the book for support. Invite them to share their thoughts with the rest of the group. Write examples of comments on the displayed photocopiable page.
● Ensure that the children understand how to fill in the whole sheet before giving each child a copy to complete.

Differentiation
For older/more confident learners: Ask the children to write profiles about characters from other popular stories.
For younger/less confident learners: Encourage the children to focus on the appearance of Grace and Nana by looking closely at the pictures in the book.

Plot, character and setting

Getting into role

> **Objective:** To act out their own and well-known stories, using voices for characters.
> **What you need:** Copies of *Amazing Grace* and dressing-up clothes suitable for teachers of both sexes.
> **Cross-curricular links:** PSHE.

What to do

● After reading *Amazing Grace,* re-read the discussion between the teacher, Grace and her school friends about who should play Peter Pan. Why did Grace's friends say that she could not play Peter? How do the children think that Grace felt when her friends made their comments? How does the teacher solve the problem of too many children wanting to play Peter?

● Suggest that the children re-enact the scene in groups, with one child in each group playing the teacher. Invite the teacher from each group to choose dressing-up clothes to put on.

● Explore the double page image of Grace and her friends responding to the teacher. Talk about the way they are sitting and their facial expressions. Encourage the groups to consider the dialogue they will use and the actions they will make in their re-enactments, for example, putting up their hands and taking turns to speak.

● Make comparisons between the re-enactments.

> **Differentiation**
> **For older/more confident learners:** Ask the children to take on the role of teacher and pose a problem for class discussion saying, for example, 'Some elderly people who live near the school are feeling lonely. What can we do to make them feel less lonely?'
> **For younger/less confident learners:** Encourage the children to role-play school scenarios by providing suitable dressing-up clothes and props.

Beginning, middle and end

> **Objective:** To read more challenging texts which can be decoded using their acquired phonic knowledge and skills, along with automatic recognition of high frequency words.
> **What you need:** Copies of *Amazing Grace,* photocopiable page 16 (one large copy and one copy for every pair of children) and scissors.

What to do

● Display the large version of photocopiable page 16 on the board and read the sentences together. Encourage the children to use their phonic knowledge and skills to tackle challenging words such as 'pantomimes'. Support them if necessary with more difficult words such as 'theatre' and 'auditions'.

● Read the sentences to the class in the order they appear on the sheet and discuss this order. Ask: *Do they tell the story in the correct sequence? Which sentence might start/finish the story?*

● Continue the discussion by asking about sentences describing events in the middle of the story.

● Ask the children to work in twos and provide each pair with a copy of photocopiable page 16 and some scissors. Tell them to cut out the sentences and put them in their chosen order.

● Ask the children to read out their sequences to the class. Are they the same or different? Which sequence tells the story most accurately? (The most probable sequence is 1, 10, 4, 6, 11, 8, 7, 3, 2, 9, 5.)

> **Differentiation**
> **For older/more confident learners:** Ask the children to write sentences on strips of paper to tell their favourite story, making sure they include a beginning, middle and end. Mix the strips up and then tell them to put them back in the correct order.
> **For younger/less confident learners:** Provide a simplified version of photocopiable page 16 with around four sentences to rearrange.

Plot, character and setting

Alternative endings

> **Objective:** To find and use new and interesting words and phrases, including story language.
> **What you need:** Copies of *Amazing Grace*, a range of traditional and contemporary storybooks and writing materials.

What to do
● Read *Amazing Grace* and then focus on the end page. Talk about how the author uses words effectively to draw the story to a satisfying conclusion, for example, 'great success', 'amazing', 'she can do anything she want'.
● Explore a range of traditional and contemporary fiction to find satisfying words and phrases for story endings, such as 'And they all lived happily ever after', 'Splash! The big bad troll sank to the bottom of the river and was never seen again!', 'There was only one home that was quite right for Harry – and that was…Harry's home'.

● Suggest that the children think of an alternative ending for *Amazing Grace*. Perhaps she could be invited to watch a West End production of *Peter Pan* or fly in an aeroplane?
● Ask the children to write their alternative ending in sentences and read them to the class.
● Discuss the endings, considering which words are most effective.
● Select the most popular ending and read it in context, instead of the final page of the book.

> **Differentiation**
> **For older/more confident learners:** Invite the children to write alternative endings to traditional stories, such as 'Little Red Riding Hood'.
> **For younger/less confident learners:** Read stories with predictable happy endings, such as 'And they all lived happily ever after'. Encourage the children to join in so that they experience the satisfaction of traditional story language.

Fun with words

> **Objective:** To explore how particular words are used, including words and expressions with similar meaning.
> **What you need:** Copies of *Amazing Grace*.

What to do
● Read *Amazing Grace*, pausing to focus on expressions the children may not understand. Read 'She was a cast of thousands' and ask the children what they think this means, if necessary read the preceding sentence, 'Grace played all the parts herself', to help them. Explain that authors sometimes use words in different ways to make their stories more interesting or exciting.
● Read the section about Grace playing the part of Doctor Grace when Ma and Nana's 'lives were in her hands'. Discuss how effective these words are in making Grace's role more dramatic.
● Explain simply that there are many ways to say the same thing, but that choosing the right

words for different contexts is most important.
● Write story linked sentences on the board and invite the children to make them more exciting by adding or changing words, while still keeping the meaning the same, for example, 'The wolf was in the wood'.
● Choose a picture book with no text and as a class make up an appropriate sentence to accompany the illustration on each page.

> **Differentiation**
> **For older/more confident learners:** Provide the children with the name of a storybook character and ask them to make up a sentence about him/her, using interesting words to bring the character to life. Compare their word choices for describing the same character.
> **For younger/less confident learners:** Provide the children with one word and a choice of three to choose the correct one from that has the same meaning, for example, 'sad' – 'happy, joyful or unhappy'.

Plot, character and setting

Word choices

> **Objective:** To make adventurous word and language choices appropriate to the style and purpose of text.
> **What you need:** Copies of *Amazing Grace*, a selection of storybooks, copies of other titles from the *Read and Respond* series for Key Stage 1, photocopiable page 17 (one large copy and one copy for each child) and writing materials.

What to do

● Look through the selection of books together and talk about how they all have different characters in them. Name some of them and ask the children to say which books they are from. Talk about how some characters, like the Large family, by Jill Murphy, appear in lots of different stories.
● Read the title, *Amazing Grace,* and discuss how the author has used one descriptive word to capture Grace's character – 'amazing'.

● Invite the children to make a list of the main characters in the books available. Choose an appropriate word to describe each character. Talk in detail about this, for example, is the Gruffalo really frightening or does he just look fierce?
● Display the large version of photocopiable page 17 and read through it so that the children understand how to complete it. Provide each child with a small copy to fill in.
● Read the children's word choices and discuss their effectiveness.

> **Differentiation**
> **For older/more confident learners:** Encourage the children to write whole sentences to capture what is special about a favourite storybook character.
> **For younger/less confident learners:** Provide the children with contrasting words to choose from to describe a well-known character, for example, Mrs Large (*Five Minutes' Peace*) – cross/patient. Encourage them to give reasons.

Audition time

> **Objective:** To present part of traditional stories, their own stories or work drawn from different parts of the curriculum for members of their own class.
> **What you need:** Copies of *Amazing Grace,* a selection of the children's favourite storybooks, fantasy costumes and props, photocopiable page 18 (one for each child) and writing materials.
> **Cross-curricular links:** Drama.

What to do

● Read *Amazing Grace* and focus on the discussion in Grace's classroom when the children tried to decide who should play Peter Pan. What did the teacher do? Introduce the word 'audition' and talk about the children's experiences of auditions. Have they ever taken part in one or seen one on a television programme? What is the role of the judges?
● Suggest that the children hold auditions for group performances of their favourite story, while

their classmates play the part of judges and give scores out of five. The group which scores highest could then perform their play to an audience of family members or at a school assembly.
● Ask the class to vote for the story they wish to perform. Then divide the class into groups, let them allocate parts and rehearse. Ensure that there are sufficient costumes and props for several groups to choose from.
● The groups take turn to perform the plays, while others write comments and scores on photocopiable page 18. Read the comment sheets together and count the votes.

> **Differentiation**
> **For older/more confident learners:** Encourage the children in groups to write a simple script to follow.
> **For younger/less confident learners:** Just allow the children to enjoy the dressing up and performing without involving judges and auditions.

Plot, character and setting

Who am I?

● Use the boxes to write down words and phrases to describe Grace and Nana. Use your ideas to write character profiles overleaf.

Grace
Appearance
Character

Nana
Appearance
Character

Illustration © 1991, Caroline Binch.

Plot, character and setting

Beginning, middle and end

● Cut out the sentences in the boxes and arrange them in the correct order to tell the story.

Grace loved to listen to her Nana telling stories.
Grace was chosen to be Peter Pan.
Grace took part in the class auditions.
Best of all Grace loved pantomimes.
Grace felt as if she could fly all the way home.
Grace wanted to be Peter Pan so she put her hand up.
Nana took Grace to the theatre to see a ballet.
Nana said Grace could do anything if she put her mind to it.
Grace was an amazing Peter Pan.
Grace dressed as Joan of Arc, Anansi and Hiawatha.
Grace's friends said she could not be Peter Pan.

Plot, character and setting

Word choices

● Put a ring round the storybook characters who do NOT appear in *Amazing Grace*.

Anansi	**Burglar Bill**	**Handa**
Joan of Arc	**Dick Whittington**	**Mowgli**
Fantastic Mr Fox	**Hannibal**	**Peter Pan**

● Write a descriptive word to describe a favourite storybook character of your choice in each of the boxes below. The first one is done for you.

Name of character   *Nana*

Descriptive word   *kind*

Name of character

Descriptive word

Name of character

Descriptive word

● Below, write a descriptive sentence to explain what is special about a friend or family member.

_____

_____

Plot, character and setting

Audition time

● Use this sheet to make short notes about each performance and give scores out of five by shading in up to five stars.

Name of group _____

Comments:

Mark out of five ☆ ☆ ☆ ☆ ☆

Name of group _____

Comments:

Mark out of five ☆ ☆ ☆ ☆ ☆

Name of group _____

Comments:

Mark out of five ☆ ☆ ☆ ☆ ☆

READ & RESPOND: Activities based on Amazing Grace

SCHOLASTIC
www.scholastic.co.uk

Talk about it

Let's be ballet dancers

> **Objective:** To explore familiar themes and characters through improvisation and role-play.
> **What you need:** Copies of *Amazing Grace*; web/poster/book images of theatres; ballet costumes such as a tutu, leotard, ballet skirt, tights (girl), T-shirt and tights (boy), ballet shoes or PE shoes (either sex); ballet music that tells a story, such as *Coppélia* by Delibes; and a book outlining the story.
> **Cross-curricular links:** Music; drama.

What to do

● Read the pages in the book about Grace and Nana going to the theatre. Ask: *What did they see? What did the outside of the theatre look like? Have you ever been to a theatre?* Invite individuals to talk about their experiences.
● Ask the children to describe the ballerina in the book. Pass around items of clothing used by ballet dancers and discuss them.
● Invite the children to lie or sit comfortably to listen to some music you are about to play. Put on contrasting ballet music, such as 'Ballade' and 'Mazurka' from Act 1 of *Coppélia*, and talk about images the children see in their minds when each one is played.
● Read the story of *Coppélia*, retell the story together, dress up in ballet costumes and make up movements to tell the story through dance.

> **Differentiation**
> **For older/more confident learners:** Retell another story through words and then dance, such as *The nutcracker* by Tchaikovsky.
> **For younger/less confident learners:** Simply allow the children to dress up and pretend to be ballet dancers enjoying moving to contrasting music.

My family support

> **Objective:** To tell stories and describe incidents from their own experience in an audible voice.
> **What you need:** Copies of *Amazing Grace*.
> **Cross-curricular links:** PSHE.

What to do

● Read the section of the book and look at the illustrations about the children in the class saying that Grace cannot be Peter Pan. Then talk about how Grace relays this conversation to her Nana and Ma and the responses they give.
● Ask questions to encourage the children's empathy: *How do you think Grace is feeling when the other children are talking and when she tells her family about it? How do Nana and Ma help Grace to manage her feelings?*
● Grace feels better after talking to Nana and Ma. Encourage the children to talk about the members of their own families that they turn to when they have problems. Ask them how the family help them to feel better – perhaps with a cuddle or a kind word.
● Ask the children if they ever help younger siblings or elderly family members when they feel sad and what they do or say to help them.
● Discuss sibling relationships. What do the children do together? Do they share games and toys? Do they ever argue? How do they resolve disagreements?
● Extend the conversation to include how families support one another in everyday situations as well as times of difficulty.

> **Differentiation**
> **For older/more confident learners:** Provide an imaginary scenario for the children to discuss, for example, a particular family member is ill. Ask: *Who will help? What will they do?*
> **For younger/less confident learners:** Encourage the children to talk simply about their families and the things that they do together.

Talk about it

Discussing feelings

Objective: To respond to presentations by describing characters, repeating some highlights and commenting constructively.
What you need: Copies of *Amazing Grace* and photocopiable page 22 (one for each child).
Cross-curricular links: PSHE.

What to do

● Read *Amazing Grace*, discussing emotions from Grace's viewpoint at significant moments, such as dressing as a favourite character, listening to comments about her suitability for Peter Pan, visiting the theatre and playing the part of Peter Pan.
● Encourage the children to think about how Grace feels when she is listening to Nana tell a story (warm, comfortable, excited, happy?). Support discussion by looking at the illustration of this event, particularly at the expression on Grace's face.

● Discuss how Grace feels when she is in different roles, such as spider Anansi weaving a wicked web or brave Joan of Arc. Again use the illustrations to support ideas.
● Consider the same events from Nana's viewpoint. Ask: *How does Nana feel as she watches her granddaughter acting? When might she be worried about her, or proud of her? How do you think she feels when she takes Grace to the theatre?*
● Extend the discussion by inviting the children to fill in photocopiable page 22 to show how we might feel in different situations.

Differentiation
For older/more confident learners: Using puppets to represent Grace and Nana, invite the children to re-enact events to demonstrate the characters' emotions.
For younger/less confident learners: Use puppets as you recount certain events in the story to make the reactions of Grace and Nana more obvious.

Watch, listen and discuss

Objective: To consider how mood and atmosphere are created in live or recorded performances.
What you need: Copies of *Amazing Grace*, video camera, audio recording equipment and playback facilities for video and audio.
Cross-curricular links: ICT.

What to do

● Read the section where Grace tells Nana and Ma how unhappy she is about the children's comments on her suitability to play Peter Pan.
● Divide the children into two groups and ask them to re-enact the scene, choosing who will play the parts, who will do the recording and who will be the audience.
● Provide video and audio equipment so that one group can record their scene using video equipment and the other using audio.
● Watch and listen to the two productions and

comment on the content as a class.
● Decide which production was the most successful and which one included the most detail.
● Talk about how different voices can enhance audio and body language can enhance video recordings. Try recording again in the light of this information and discuss the results.
● Change equipment over so that the groups have a chance to try both methods of recording.

Differentiation
For older/more confident learners: Make an audio recording of the children retelling a story involving lots of voice changes, such as 'The Three Little Pigs'. Discuss the success of the production.
For younger/less confident learners: Make a video recording of the children re-enacting a favourite story involving lots of movement, such as 'The Enormous Turnip', and then have fun watching it together.

Talk about it

Story language

> **Objective:** To tell real or imagined stories using the conventions of familiar story language.
> **What you need:** Copies of *Amazing Grace*, photocopiable page 23 (one for each child) and a selection of favourite stories.

What to do

● Read *Amazing Grace* and ask the children to look through the selection of storybooks for examples of story language. Make a list of 'story words' together, such as 'Once upon a time' and 'Happily ever after'. Then move on to talk about how all stories have a beginning, middle and end.
● Return to *Amazing Grace* and talk about what happens at the beginning, middle and end of the story.
● Provide each child with a copy of photocopiable page 23 to complete. Ask them to decide if the

phrases come from the beginning, middle or end of a story, then draw a line to the correct box. They should be as follows: Beginning – Once upon a time, At first, A long time ago there lived; Middle – And then, After that, By and by; End – Happily ever after, In the end.
● Use the completed lists to help to write a story, either to make up a new one or to retell a well-known one.

> **Differentiation**
> **For older/more confident learners:** Invite individuals to read their completed stories aloud and discuss how they can be developed or extended.
> **For younger/less confident learners:** Use the story language as you re-enact a simple traditional story with the class. Encourage the children to emphasise the beginning and end of the story with phrases, such as 'Once upon a time' and 'Happily ever after'.

Favourite stories

> **Objective:** To engage with books through exploring and enacting interpretations.
> **What you need:** Copies of *Amazing Grace*; books telling traditional and pantomime stories mentioned in *Amazing Grace*; everyday props similar to those used by Grace (such as a broom, tights, a cardboard box, a bag, a stick and a bicycle pump) and photocopiable page 24 (one for each child).
> **Cross-curricular links:** History; ICT.

What to do

● Talk about the everyday items Grace uses as props when she pretends to be the characters featured in the story.
● Provide each child with a copy of photocopiable page 24 to complete. Encourage them to refer to the text and illustrations of *Amazing Grace* to help them with sentence content. The answers are: lamp, horse, Juliet, Joan and Dick.

● Read some of the books of traditional and pantomime stories and discuss the links with *Amazing Grace*.
● Invite the children to work in groups, with each group selecting an event from one of the stories to dramatise. Use clothes and props to enhance the dramatisation for the rest of the class.

> **Differentiation**
> **For older/more confident learners:** In pairs encourage the children to use websites and books to find out more about historical characters featuring in the story, such as Joan of Arc and Hannibal. Invite them to share these facts with the rest of the class.
> **For younger/less confident learners:** Invite the children to choose a picture of a character that Grace dresses up as, and draw their own interpretation. Help them find out more about the character's life from books so that they can enhance their illustration.

SECTION
5

Discussing feelings

● Read the sentences in each box and ring the face that matches your reaction. Then write sentences describing how you would feel.

Someone has pushed you over in the playground and you have cut your knee.
Your friend has asked you to come and play after school.
You are lost in the woods and there is nobody else there.
Your puppy is ill and you are taking him to the vet.
You have lost your favourite toy and cannot find it anywhere.
It is your birthday today.

Story language

● The phrases on the left are all common in stories. Read each one and then draw a line to where it should fit into a story – the beginning, the middle or the end.

Once upon a time	
Happily ever after	**Beginning**
And then	
At first	
In the end	**Middle**
After that	
A long time ago there lived	**End**
By and by	

Talk about it

Favourite stories

- Read the sentences about Grace's favourite stories and fill in the missing words. The words are at the bottom of the sheet.

Grace had a shiny — — — — that she rubbed when she was Aladdin.

Grace made a wooden — — — — — out of a box and hid inside.

Grace pretended to be Mowgli and crawled around the big garden — — — — — .

Nana took Grace to see Romeo and — — — — — .

Grace loved to dress up as — — — — of Arc and fight big battles.

Juliet   jungle   lamp   Joan   horse

SCHOLASTIC
www.scholastic.co.uk

READ & RESPOND: Activities based on Amazing Grace

Get writing

Doctor Grace makes a visit

> **Objective:** To use question marks and use commas to separate items.
> **What you need:** Copies of *Amazing Grace* and photocopiable page 28 (one large copy and one copy for each child).

What to do

● Explore the double page showing Grace in role as a doctor treating Nana and Ma. Ask: *What do you think is wrong with Ma? Why is Doctor Grace treating her? What has she done with the bandages? Why is Nana holding her head? What do you think Grace is using the wooden spoon and rope for? Why do Nana and Ma have their feet up on a table?*

● Encourage the children to think about the dialogue between the characters. What questions might Grace ask to find out what is wrong with her patients? How might they respond?

● Display an enlarged copy of photocopiable page 28 and read through Grace's questions together. Invite the children to suggest responses for both Nana and Ma.

● Now read the responses on the displayed photocopiable page and ask the children to think about what the questions might have been to result in such responses.

● Finally, explain how the children should make Grace's list of treatments for Nana into one sentence, separated by commas.

● Provide each child with a copy of photocopiable page 28 to complete.

> **Differentiation**
> **For older/more confident learners:** Invite the children to make up and write a short dialogue between Grace and Nana to fit the context of the illustration.
> **For younger/less confident learners:** Take on the role of doctor and encourage interaction with child 'patients'. Model the writing of a prescription and provide resources for the children to continue the role-play.

Book review

> **Objective:** To group written sentences together in chunks of meaning or subject.
> **What you need:** Several copies of *Amazing Grace*, photocopiable page 29 (one large copy and one copy for each child) and a selection of the children's favourite books.

What to do

● Read *Amazing Grace* together and discuss how the book is presented, commenting on layout, illustrations and text.

● Invite the children to talk about their favourite part of the story. Ask if they think Grace is a suitable main character and why.

● Explain the purpose of a book review and read a few examples of reviews from the covers of the children's favourite books, drawing attention to the type of information given. Ask the children to write a book review for *Amazing Grace*.

● Display an enlarged copy of photocopiable page 29 and read through the instructions and headings together. Encourage the children to discuss their likes and dislikes about the story to motivate the use of adventurous language and ideas when writing sentences on their sheets and writing their reviews.

● Provide each child with a copy of photocopiable page 29 to use for writing notes before creating their own *Amazing Grace* reviews.

> **Differentiation**
> **For older/more confident learners:** Invite the children to choose another story to write a review about, using the photocopiable page for notes.
> **For younger/less confident learners:** Focus on one aspect of *Amazing Grace*, such as a particular event or character. Ask the children to draw a picture and write a caption about their chosen focus.

Get writing

Guess who?

> **Objective:** To convey information and ideas in simple non-narrative forms.
> **What you need:** Copies of *Amazing Grace*, A4 card and photocopiable page 30 (one large copy and one copy for every child).

What to do

● Display a large copy of photocopiable page 30, ensuring you cover up the character's names, and invite the children to name the three characters illustrated and their identifying features. For example, Dick Whittington's stick and tied handkerchief.

● Invite them to suggest words to link with the illustrations, for example, 'brave', 'army leader', 'France' and 'Saint' to describe Joan of Arc.

● Discuss famous characters the children might draw in the empty box and appropriate words they might use to describe this character.

● Provide each child with a copy of photocopiable page 30 and card to glue each picture to. While the glue is drying, encourage them to make a note of words to put on the back of the cards they are making.

● Once dry, ask the children to cut out their cards and complete them as directed.

● In pairs, ask them to play a guessing game with one child reading out the words (shielding the actual illustration), while the other guesses which character is being described/represented.

> **Differentiation**
> **For older/more confident learners:** Invite the children to make a matching game by creating two cards respresenting each character in the game – one illustrating the character and the other an object associated with that character. Then play the game.
> **For younger/less confident learners:** Write a character's name on a sheet of paper and encourage the children to draw a picture of someone wearing a suitable costume underneath.

Amazing words

> **Objective:** To spell new words using phonics as the prime approach.
> **What you need:** Copies of *Amazing Grace*, books about different 'amazing' characters such as *Mr Majeika* by Humphrey Carpenter (Puffin), *Amazing Mr Zooty* by Emma Chichester Clark (Andersen Press) and *My Amazing Dad* by Ross Collins (Young Puffin).

What to do

● Read *Amazing Grace* and then discuss the title. Ask: *Why is Grace 'amazing'? What does 'amazing' mean?*

● Read some stories about characters who are amazing and talk about their special talents.

● Discuss the difference between a real 'amazing' talent, for example, that of a great musician, and an imaginary one, such as Mr Majeika's ability to fly around on a magic carpet.

● Invite the children to invent an amazing character of their own and encourage discussion about whether the talent is real or imaginary.

● Encourage the children to put their inventions on paper to make a class book entitled *Amazing Characters*, with each child contributing a page.

● While the children are writing and illustrating their pages, encourage them to try to spell words using their acquired knowledge of phonics.

> **Differentiation**
> **For older/more confident learners:** Invite the children to use dressing-up clothes and props to bring their invented 'amazing' characters to life in a short dramatisation.
> **For younger/less confident learners:** Ask the children to draw a picture of their character, prompting them with appropriate questions. Support them as they write, or scribe a sentence for them, about why their character is amazing.

Get writing

Poster design

> **Objective:** To select from different presentational features to suit particular writing purposes on paper and on screen.
> **What you need:** Copies of *Amazing Grace* and examples of posters and leaflets advertising theatre productions, shows, galleries, cinemas and so forth.
> **Cross-curricular links:** Drama.

What to do

● Read *Amazing Grace* and focus on the pages about Grace's theatre visit. Draw attention to signs and posters outside the theatre and discuss the information they give. Point to and explain words such as 'stunning new Juliet' and 'matinee'. Ask: *Who is playing Juliet? How do we know?* Talk about the use of different types of lettering and illustrations.
● With parental permission, visit a theatre, cinema or art gallery with small groups of children to look at advertising displays and pick up leaflets about forthcoming productions and events.
● Back in your setting, explore the posters and leaflets, and ask questions about their content.
● On a large sheet of paper or board make a list of things the children would like to include on a poster advertising a class dramatisation of *Amazing Grace*, such as production title, times, dates, names of stars and a short review.
● Create the poster together and hang it up in a prominent position for parents to see.

> **Differentiation**
> **For older/more confident learners:** Invite the children to create individual mini-posters to take home inviting parents to the production.
> **For younger/less confident learners:** Ask the children to illustrate the main characters in the story and write their names underneath. Use their drawings in a large wall display about the production.

Writing a sequel

> **Objective:** To explain their reactions to texts, commenting on important aspects.
> **What you need:** Copies of *Amazing Grace*.
> **Cross-curricular links:** PSHE.

What to do

● Read *Amazing Grace* and then discuss what the text tells us about the things that Grace likes to do. Remembering these things, ask what the children think might happen to Grace when she grows up. Perhaps she might become a famous dancer such as Rosalie from Trinidad who took the part of Juliet in the ballet production.
● Introduce the word 'ambition' and explain that it was Grace's ambition to play the part of Peter Pan in the school play. Talk about the children's ambitions. What would they really like to do if they could choose anything? Encourage them to be adventurous in their thinking.
● Explain that many books have 'sequels' and that a sequel is a book that follows another. If we read a sequel to *Amazing Grace* we would discover what happens to her in the future. Encourage the children to let their imaginations help them to write their own short sequels to the story.
● Invite the children to read out their sequels, look for similarities and differences, and decide which one is the most unusual.

> **Differentiation**
> **For older/more confident learners:** Recall the discussion about ambition, and ask the children to write about a special ambition and how they might fulfil it.
> **For younger/less confident learners:** Help the children to voice their thoughts about what might happen to Grace next by careful questioning. Support them as they write these thoughts down.

SECTION
6

Doctor Grace makes a visit

● Read each of Grace's questions and write her patient's answers in a sentence in the empty boxes below.

Can you tell me what the problem is?
Can you describe your aches and pains to me?
Have you taken any medicine?

● Now read some patients' answers and write suitable questions to match them.

I fell over on the path and now my ankle is hurting when I walk.
My head is aching and my throat is sore.

● Here is a list of things that Grace wrote down to help Nana get better. Put them all into one sentence. (Remember to use a capital letter, commas and a full stop.)

take this tablet   **close your eyes**

sit on a chair   **have a rest**

put your feet up on a stool

READ & RESPOND: Activities based on Amazing Grace

Book review

- Use this sheet to help you to plan and write a book review for *Amazing Grace*.

Write a sentence describing what *Amazing Grace* is about.

_____

_____

Characters
Circle the words you could use to describe Grace in your review:

lazy   determined   brave   cross   strong

unfriendly   imaginative   shy   pretty   clever

- Write a sentence describing what you like about *Amazing Grace*.

_____

_____

- Write a sentence describing what you dislike about *Amazing Grace*.

_____

_____

- Give the story a rating out of five by shading in the stars.

Get writing

Guess who?

● Cut out each picture and on the back, write some words or phrases that describe each character mentioned in *Amazing Grace*. Your partner has to guess who the character is. In the empty box draw your own famous story character and describe them.

Dick Whittington	Aladdin

	Joan of Arc

READ & RESPOND: Activities based on *Amazing Grace*

Illustration © 2009, Jon Mitchell/Beehive Illustration.

Assessment

Assessment advice

Ongoing formative assessments of individual achievements and progress in literacy are an essential component of the planning and assessment cycle. They help teachers to make valuable judgements about a child's progress towards specific learning targets, and also to ensure that future learning activities are planned at an appropriate level. Assessment outcomes are invaluable in determining new individual targets. Reports and assessments should be based on clear evidence arising from observations and examples of actual work completed.

Formative assessments build up gradually and should be created from a variety of sources, such as observations, contributions to classroom discussions, peer group interaction and analysis of the children's practical work. The importance of peer- and self-assessment should not be overlooked. All of the activities in this book can be assessed using a combination of these methods.

Each activity in the book has a clear assessable learning objective which represents what a child should know, or be able to do, by the end of that activity. Informing the children of these objectives before an activity begins is essential in order to help them to recognise their involvement in their own learning. Likewise, at the end of each activity there should be a time for reflection when the children can revisit the learning objective and discuss whether or not they feel they have achieved it. This helps them to understand the significance of assessment in planning the next steps in learning.

You can use the assessment activity on photocopiable page 32 as part of a record of individual progress and it is a useful tool for assessing a child's story-writing ability.

Amazing story plan

> **Assessment focus:** To draw on knowledge and experience of texts in deciding and planning what and how to write.
> **What you need:** Copies of *Amazing Grace*, photocopiable page 32 (one large copy and one copy for each child) and writing materials.

What to do
● Read *Amazing Grace* to the children and talk about the story.
● Display the enlarged copy of photocopiable page 32 and explain that this sheet will help them to plan out a story before writing it. Read and answer the questions together in relation to the story of *Amazing Grace*.
● Suggest that the children think of an 'amazing' story of their own and provide each child with a copy of photocopiable page 32 to write a plan for it.

● While the children are making their notes, interact with individuals to support their ideas and ensure that they include notes about characters, setting and events. Encourage them to consider what happens at the beginning, middle and end of the story.
● Invite the children to write out their stories in complete sentences, using their written plans to help them.

> **Differentiation**
> **For older/more confident learners:** Encourage the children to be adventurous with vocabulary and to add descriptive words and speech to bring characters, setting and plot to life.
> **For younger/less confident learners:** Talk through ideas with individuals and suggest that they draw pictures to illustrate a significant event at the beginning, middle and end of their story. Help them with writing a caption for each picture.

Amazing story plan

● Use this sheet to plan your own amazing story.

What is the title of the story? _____

What are the names of the main characters?

_____

Where is the story set? _____

Why is the story amazing? _____

_____

What happens at the beginning of the story?

_____

_____

What happens in the middle of the story? Make sure that you write the main events here.

_____

_____

How does the story end?

_____